19

LET'S FIND OUT ABOUT

Hindu Mandirs

Anita Ganeri

JAN 23 2006

© Copyright 2006 Raintree
Published by Raintree,
a division of Reed Elsevier Inc.
Chicago, IL 60602

Customer Service 888-363-4266
Visit our website at www.raintreelibrary.com

For more information address the publisher:
Raintree, 100 N. LaSalle, Suite 1200, Chicago,
IL 60602

Editorial: Dan Nunn and Sarah Chappelow
Design: Ron Kamen and Philippa Baile
Picture research: Hannah Taylor and Sally Claxton
Production: Duncan Gilbert
Religious consultant: Yogesh Patel, Shri
  Swaminarayan Mandir, Neasden, United
  Kingdom

Originated by Modern Age
Printed in China
  by WKT Company Limited

10 09 08 07 06
10 9 8 7 6 5 4 3 2 1

**Library of Congress Cataloging-in-Publication
Data**
Ganeri, Anita, 1961-
  Hindu mandirs / Anita Ganeri.
    p. cm. -- (Let's find out about)
  Includes bibliographical references and index.
  ISBN 1-4034-7033-2
  1. Temples, Hindu--Juvenile literature.
  2. Hinduism--Juvenile literature.
  I. Title. II. Series.
  BL1243.74.G36 2005
  294.5'35--dc22
                    2005001563

Acknowledgments
The publishers would like to thank the following for
permission to reproduce photographs:

Alamy Images p. **5** (Dan Atkin); Circa Photo
Library pp. **9 bottom** (John Smith), **12** (B. J.
Mistry), **14** (William Holtby), **15** (John Smith), **17**
(John Smith), **20** (B. J. Mistry), **21** (B. J. Mistry),
22 (Robyn Beeche), **23** (John Smith), **25** (William
Holtby), **27** (Ged Murray); Corbis pp. **7** (Historical
Picture Archive), **9 top** (Dave G. Houser), **18** (Earl
& Nazima Kowall), **19** (David H. Wells); Trip pp. **4**
(J. Wakelin), **6** (R. Graham), **8** (Dinodia), **10**
(H. Rogers), **11** (H. Rogers), **13 bottom** (F. Good),
13 top (Adina Tovy), **16 bottom** (H. Rogers), **16** top
(J. Wakelin), **24** (H. Rogers), **26** (H. Rogers).

Cover photograph of the Swaminarayan Mandir in
Neasden in the United Kingdom reproduced with
permission of Trip/Adina Tovy.

Every effort has been made to contact copyright
holders of any material reproduced in this book. Any
omissions will be rectified in subsequent printings if
notice is given to the publishers.

The paper used to print this book comes from
sustainable resources.

3 9082 10012 6252

Contents

Some words are shown in bold, **like this**. You can find out what they mean by looking in the glossary. Religious words are listed with a pronunciation guide on page 29.

What Is a Mandir?

A mandir is a place where Hindus go to **worship**. It is also sometimes called a **temple**. Each mandir is **dedicated** to a particular god, goddess, or another **holy** person. For Hindus, mandirs represent God's presence on Earth. The mandir is God's home on Earth.

This Hindu mandir is in Little India, Singapore.

4

The mandir is not only a place for worship. It is also somewhere Hindus can meet their friends and learn more about their religion.

Some Hindus try to visit the mandir every day. Others only visit the mandir on special occasions, such as family celebrations and festivals. There are no strict rules.

Did You Know

Ancient rules describe how a mandir should be designed and built. Many mandirs in India follow these rules. But in other countries, such as the United Kingdom and the United States, many mandirs have been set up in buildings like churches or school halls.

Hindu women greet each other in a mandir in the United Kingdom.

5

Hindus and Hinduism

Hindus follow a religion called **Hinduism**. Hinduism is one of the oldest religions in the world. It began at least 5,000 years ago in the northern part of the modern countries of India and Pakistan.

Hindus can follow their religion in many different ways. But most Hindus share the same basic beliefs. They call their religion *sanatana dharma*, which means "eternal truth."

Thousands of years ago, the people of this ruined city worshiped gods similar to the Hindu gods of today.

6

Many Hindus believe in a great **spirit**. They call this spirit "Brahman." Brahman cannot be seen but is in everything. Some Hindus call Brahman "God."

Hindus also **worship** many other gods and goddesses. These show Brahman's special qualities and powers.

The Hindu god Indra has been important since ancient times.

Did You Know

Hindus believe that every living thing has a **soul**. When you die, your soul is born again in another body. This may be a human, an animal, or a plant. You can be reborn again and again. Hindus try to lead good lives to end the cycle of rebirth. Then their souls can become one with Brahman.

7

Mandirs from the Outside

This amazing building is the gateway to an enormous mandir in southern India.

Mandirs come in many different sizes, styles, and shapes. In India, village **temples** are usually simple buildings, about the size of a tool shed. But some **ancient** mandirs are much larger. They are like whole villages. They have shops, schools, and rooms for the **priests** to sleep in.

Most mandirs are surrounded by walls to separate the **holy** space inside from the everyday world outside. A gateway or porch opens into a hall that leads to the main **shrine**. A tall tower, called a shikhara, usually stands directly above the main shrine. It represents a **sacred** mountain, carrying people's wishes and prayers up to heaven.

8

The outside of a mandir is often beautifully decorated with carvings of gods and goddesses and sacred signs and symbols. These are to make all parts of the mandir holy.

A Hindu View

I go to the mandir in my village on my way to school. It's a very peaceful place. It makes me feel happy for the rest of the day.

—Manju, age ten, India

Some mandirs are decorated with beautiful carvings. This one is in Malibu, California.

Indian village temples are often no bigger than a room.

Mandirs from the Inside

The **holiest** part of the mandir is the main **shrine**. This is where the **sacred** images, called murtis, stand. The murtis show the gods and goddesses of the mandir. They also show God's presence on Earth.

Around the sides of the main shrine are smaller shrines. This part of the mandir is a quiet, peaceful place.

These are the sacred images from a mandir in Amritsar, India. They show the Hindu gods Rama and Sita.

10

In **Hinduism**, the gods and goddesses are often shown with several heads or arms. These show their many special qualities and powers. The most important Hindu gods are Brahma, the creator of the world; Vishnu, the protector; and Shiva, the destroyer.

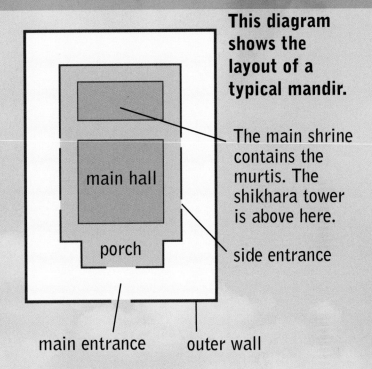

This diagram shows the layout of a typical mandir.

main hall

porch

The main shrine contains the murtis. The shikhara tower is above here.

side entrance

main entrance

outer wall

Did You Know

Many signs and symbols are used to decorate mandirs. The om symbol (pictured right) shows a sacred sound that stands for the universe. It is said at the start of prayers, **meditation**, and readings from the sacred texts.

11

Mandirs Around the World

Today, there are mandirs all over the world. Varanasi in India is the Hindus' **holiest** city. Every year, millions of Hindus come to **worship** in its thousands of mandirs and **shrines**. The most **sacred** is the Golden Mandir. It is **dedicated** to Lord Shiva and gets its name from its gold-covered tower.

Some Hindus believe that the Golden Mandir in Varanasi is a direct path to heaven.

The Swaminarayan Mandir in Neasden, London was built in 1995. To help raise money, local Hindu children collected thousands of aluminum cans for recycling.

Another beautiful mandir is in Neasden, London, in the United Kingdom. It is dedicated to an **incarnation** of God called Lord Swaminarayan. The mandir was built in a traditional style. It is covered with delicate carvings.

Did You Know

One of the largest Hindu mandirs is the Balaji Mandir in Tirupati, southern India. It has more than 25,000 visitors a day. Sometimes worshipers have to stand in line for twelve hours to reach the main shrine!

The Balaji Mandir in Tirupati is dedicated to Lord Venkateswara, who is said to grant wishes.

13

Worshiping in a Mandir

Hindus do not just visit a mandir to pray. They go to see the **sacred** images in the main **shrine**. They take offerings of flowers, fruit, sweets, and **incense** for the images. These offerings are called prasad.

The **priest** takes the prasad and offers them to the images to be **blessed** by God. Then, he gives part of them back to the **worshipers** to give them God's blessing. This way of worshiping is called **puja**.

A priest offers prasad to the sacred images at a Hindu shrine.

Another ceremony is called **arti**. The priest takes a tray of lamps and waves it in a circle in front of the sacred images to be blessed by God. As he does this, the worshipers sing a song of praise. Then they pass their hands over the flames and touch their foreheads with the warmth.

A Hindu View

Puja is our way of showing love and devotion for God. After puja in the mandir, the priest marks our foreheads with a red mark and a few rice grains. This is a sign of God's blessing.

—*Krishna Das, a Hindu living in Singapore*

This arti ceremony is taking place at a mandir in the United Kingdom.

15

Being in a Mandir

When Hindus visit a mandir, they show great care and respect. They take their shoes off and women may also cover their heads. Then, the **worshipers** ring the mandir bell. Hindus believe that they are guests of the gods and goddesses. Ringing the bell shows that they have arrived.

These worshipers at a mandir in Singapore are taking off their shoes before going inside.

Ringing the mandir bell is a way of showing respect for the gods and goddesses of the mandir.

16

People may then walk slowly around the main **shrine**. They always walk in a clockwise direction, keeping their right hands facing the shrine and the **sacred** images. This is because Hindus traditionally use their right hands for clean tasks, such as eating. They use their left hands for dirty tasks, such as washing.

A Hindu View

When we visit the mandir, we like to show respect for God. But that doesn't mean that mandirs are quiet and solemn places. They are usually full of the sound of people singing songs, chanting from the **holy** books, and ringing the mandir bell!

—Dinesh Tantia,
Chicago, Illinois

Many women cover their heads when they worship at a mandir.

17

Who Works in a Mandir?

Every mandir has its own **priest**, and larger mandirs have a whole team. The priest performs **puja**. He also helps people read and study the **sacred** books.

One of the priest's duties is to take care of the sacred images as if they are special guests. In the morning, the priest wakes the images up, washes them, dresses them, and offers them food. The images rest in the afternoon. In the evening, the priest dresses them in their nightclothes so they can go to sleep.

Priests, such as this man, play an important role in Hindu mandirs.

These priests are reading the sacred texts at a mandir in India.

It takes many other people to run a large mandir. They help in the mandir shop and make food for **worshipers**. The **volunteers** believe that this is a way of showing their love for God.

A Hindu View

I live in the mandir with the other priests. This is a large mandir so there is always plenty for us to do. Among many other duties, we perform puja and help people to learn more about **Hinduism**.
—*Priest at Pashupatinath Mandir, Kathmandu, Nepal*

19

Special Events

Special times in a Hindu's life are celebrated by the whole family. Many of these celebrations take place in the mandir. **Priests** from the mandir also visit people at home to perform different ceremonies.

When some Hindu boys are about ten, they are given a **sacred** thread by their father or a priest. It is looped over the boy's left shoulder and under his right arm. After this, the boy counts as an adult. He must wear the thread for the rest of his life.

The sacred thread ceremony is an important moment for many Hindu boys.

Did You Know ?

When a Hindu baby is born, a priest draws up a horoscope. This shows the position of the stars and planets on the baby's birthday. It is used later in life to decide lucky dates for weddings and other celebrations.

This priest is drawing up a horoscope for a newborn baby.

Many Hindu weddings take place at home, but some couples visit the mandir to be **blessed**. The most important part of the ceremony is when the couple takes seven steps together around the sacred fire. At each step, they make a promise to each other.

21

Festivals

Some Hindu festivals celebrate important times in the lives of the gods and goddesses. Others mark certain times of the year, such as springtime. At festival times, Hindus visit the mandir for **puja**. There is often music, dancing, or a special meal. People may also give sweets and gifts to each other.

The Holi festival is a time for having fun!

Holi is a spring festival. On the first day, people build bonfires and burn models of a wicked witch named Holika. The next day, they wear their old clothes and throw colored powder on each other.

These Hindus are performing a special arti ceremony to celebrate Divali.

At Divali, Hindus remember the story of Lord Rama. He won a great battle against an evil demon king. Hindus decorate the mandir and their homes with rows of tiny lamps. The lamps are said to drive away evil and welcome Lord Rama home.

A Hindu View

My favorite festival is Divali. On Saturday night, we go to the mandir for a special feast and fireworks. We also get loads of presents and some new clothes to wear.
—*Sanjay Kumar, age nine, United Kingdom*

23

Mandirs and the Community

Hindus do not only go to the mandir to **worship**. They can also meet up with their family and friends. They come to chat, celebrate special occasions, and learn more about their religion. Some big mandirs have large prayer halls with space for hundreds of worshipers. They may also have sports halls, marriage halls, and libraries.

Did You Know
Some mandirs have their own shops that sell snacks, sweets, and vegetables. Some also have kitchens where meals are cooked for worshipers.

Outside many mandirs, there are stalls selling flower garlands and other offerings.

24

Hindu children learn Sanskrit so they can read the sacred texts.

Some mandirs run classes where people can learn to read and study the Hindu **sacred** books. Many of these books are written in an **ancient** Indian language called Sanskrit. It is very difficult to learn. Sometimes the **priests** give lectures about the sacred texts. Afterward, people have the chance to talk about what they have heard and to ask questions.

Hinduism at Home

Most Hindus **worship** at home as well as at a mandir. They have a special place, sometimes called a **shrine**, set aside for **puja**. Here, the family makes offerings to **sacred** images or pictures of the family's favorite gods or goddesses. They always take off their shoes before they go near the shrine, just as they do in the mandir.

Most Hindus have small shrines at home where they can perform puja.

As part of their daily worship, a family might perform the **arti** ceremony twice a day in the morning and evening. At special times, such as festivals, they peform a longer puja. In some homes, people offer their food to the god or goddess before they eat it. This means that the food is **blessed** by God.

Many Hindu families pray together at home every day.

A Hindu View

We are lucky because we have a puja room at home. It is very peaceful and beautiful with the images of the gods. I say my prayers here every morning and evening.
—*Arti Agarwal, Kolkata, India*

27

Hinduism Around the World

Hinduism is the world's third biggest religion. There are about one billion Hindus. Most still live in India, where Hinduism began. Hindus also live in the neighboring Asian countries of Nepal, Bhutan, Pakistan, Sri Lanka, Bangladesh, and Myanmar. Some live in parts of Southeast Asia such as Malaysia and Indonesia.

More recently, Hindus have settled in the United Kingdom, Australia, Canada, and the United States. Many Hindus have lived there all their lives, but their religion is still very important. There are hundreds of mandirs in these countries where Hindus can **worship**.

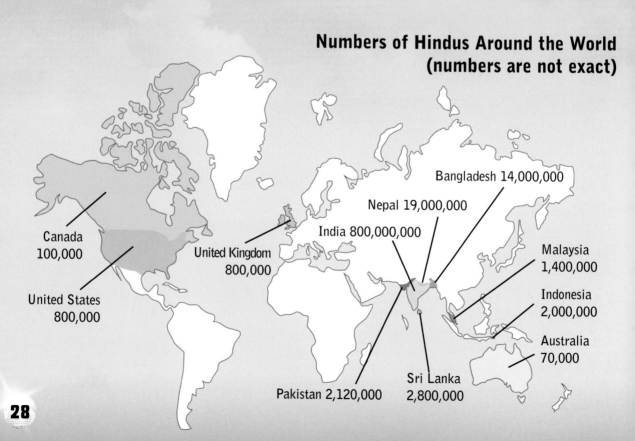

**Numbers of Hindus Around the World
(numbers are not exact)**

Canada 100,000
United States 800,000
United Kingdom 800,000
India 800,000,000
Nepal 19,000,000
Bangladesh 14,000,000
Malaysia 1,400,000
Indonesia 2,000,000
Australia 70,000
Sri Lanka 2,800,000
Pakistan 2,120,000

Useful Words

These are some of the religious words that have been used in this book. You can find out how to say them by reading the pronunciation guide in the brackets after each word.

arti [ar-tee] – part of Hindu worship in which a tray of lamps is waved in front of murtis as a way of welcoming them

Brahma [bruh-maa] – one of the three most important Hindu gods; the creator of the world

Brahman [bruh-mun] – the great soul or spirit who cannot be seen but is present in everything

Divali [dee-waa-lee] – the Hindu festival of light, celebrated in October or November

Hindu [hin-doo] – to do with Hinduism, or someone who follows the Hindu religion

Holi [ho-lee] – an important Hindu festival, celebrated in spring

mandir [mun-deer] – a place where Hindus worship

murti [moor-tee] – a sacred image of a god, goddess, or holy person

om [om] – a sacred symbol and sound that stands for the universe

prasad [pru-shaad] – food, offered to the gods, then shared out with worshipers

puja [poo-jaa] – Hindu worship

sanatana dharma [sun-aat-unu dhur-mu] – the eternal truth; the name Hindus give to their beliefs

Sanskrit [saan-skrit] – an ancient Indian language

shikhara [shik-aara] – the tall tower of a Hindu mandir

Shiva [shi-vuh] – one of the three most important Hindu gods; the destroyer of the world

Vishnu [vish-noo] – one of the three most important Hindu gods; the protector of the world

Glossary

ancient very old

arti part of Hindu worship in which a tray of lamps is waved in front of sacred images as a way of welcoming them

bless ask God to take care of someone or something

dedicate when a mandir is dedicated to a god or goddess, it belongs to that god or goddess

Hinduism set of beliefs followed by Hindus

holy to do with God or belonging to God

incarnation when God appears on Earth in human form

incense sweet-smelling spices that are burned as offerings to God

meditation sitting quietly and focusing your mind to gain inner calm and peace

priest religious person who carries out puja (Hindu worship)

puja Hindu worship

sacred another word for holy

shrine part of a mandir where the sacred images stand

soul word used for the thinking, feeling part of a person, rather than the physical body

spirit another word for soul

temple place of worship. A mandir is sometimes called a temple.

volunteer person who works without being paid

worship way of praising and remembering God

Finding Out More

Visiting a Mandir

Many Hindu mandirs welcome visitors, as long as they follow certain rules of behavior. Visitors should phone the mandir in advance and arrange a time to visit. They should ask if it is possible to see the sacred images (in some mandirs, only Hindus are allowed into the main shrine).

As with all holy places, people must treat the mandir with care and respect. Visitors should dress respectfully. For example, they should not wear a short skirt, shorts, or have bare shoulders. When they arrive at the mandir, they should take off their shoes. Women and girls may also be expected to cover their heads. Visitors should not take food and drink inside the mandir, unless they are meant as offerings.

Visitors may be able to take photographs outside the mandir but probably not inside. It is always best to ask permission first. To say thank-you for their visit, visitors could make a donation to the mandir.

More Books to Read

Ganeri, Anita. *Celebrations: Divali*. Chicago: Heinemann Library, 2002.

Parker, Victoria. *The Ganges and Other Hindu Holy Places*. Chicago: Raintree, 2003.

Penney, Sue. *Hinduism*. Chicago: Heinemann Library, 2001.

Index